Living Beyond Existence

Kirby's Gift from the Afterlife

This is a True Story

Bryon Richard Smith
and
Shannon Amy Smith

Dedication

I dedicate

Living Beyond Existence
Kirby's Gift from the Afterlife

To my cousin Kirby
whose life was tragically cut short

All who knew him were deeply affected by his death
And we all still miss and love him very much

Kirby Raymond Smith
1964-1981

Introduction

What you are about to read will become controversial and will spark many debates. It will cause people to question their own beliefs and may even offend them in the process. *Living Beyond Existence-Kirby's Gift from the Afterlife* will become a new religion to some and heresy to others. Neither was my intention. My goal is simply to tell the story of three people—my cousin Kirby, my wife Shannon, and myself—and the incredible message Kirby brought to me one night in October, a message from the afterlife through my wife, Shannon, a psychic medium.

I'd waited my entire life for this message, and yet I was not quite prepared for it, because it turned out to be so much more than I expected. The knowledge in this book may answer your questions about the afterlife, what it is, what it means, and what our purpose is on the other side of existence. Surprisingly, you might also glimpse into what our purpose is here in this life, and the connection between the two sides of existence. So if you are a nonbeliever or someone who is discouraged with traditional religions and is looking for something more to believe in, then suspend your disbelief and take a leap of faith into destiny, for it may just lead you to a new outlook on both your life here and your afterlife, an insight that could forever change your fate.

Bryon Richard Smith

Kirby's Gift from the Afterlife

Table of Contents

This book is for people who believe in impossible

possibilities.

Shannon Amy Smith

Chapter One

Kirby's Gift

I am riding with my cousin Kirby in his Datsun 260z. We are young, laughing, and excited about life, both seventeen years old with our future ahead of us. All of a sudden we crash through the guardrail and plunge down the cliff toward our deaths. In the split second before we hit bottom, I'm jolted awake by my fear, out of a nightmare that leaves me covered in sweat. I begin to cry, praying to God this was just a nightmare and not a premonition of what's to come. It is mid April 1981, and I tell no one of the dream.

Fast forward to October 1, 1981, a mere six months later, when I am awakened out of a deep sleep by my distraught mother telling me that Kirby has been in a car accident, his 260z crashed as he fought for his life. No one could say whether he would live or die. From that moment on, my life would never be the same. Kirby had suffered a severe head injury along with other lesser injuries, but the damage to his brain posed the great threat to his life.

My family drove from our home in Fremont to Chico, a small college town near where the accident occurred. Kirby had been taken to the local hospital where he clung to life. Kirby's schoolmate was driving Kirby's car and drifted into a guardrail end cap on the side of the road. The driver was killed instantly and Kirby was thrown forward into the dashboard, causing the head injury that put him in a coma. Unfortunately no one was wearing seat belts.

For the next several days we huddled in the hallways of the hospital, his friends and family praying for Kirby to live. But, on October 4th, Sunday afternoon, Kirby passed away and with him passed a lifetime of happiness for all who knew him. My whole family was so grief stricken because Kirby was the kind of person to whom people were drawn. He had a great sense of humor that was one of a kind, infectious. He was more than a good kid, he was my best friend and he was one of those rare people you meet in life and are better for it, and now he was gone.

There in the hospital just after Kirby's passing and in the midst of all the crying, no one noticed I had run off. Not knowing where I was going I somehow found myself outside the door to the hospital chapel. It offered me a chance for some privacy, to be alone with my grief, so I entered an extremely small room. But it offered me solitude, or so I thought. As I sat there crying and asking God why this happened I had an overwhelming feeling I was no longer alone. No one had entered the chapel, yet I felt I was surrounded by a divine entity, I felt it was God, I felt certain of it, and suddenly my eyes dried up and I could not cry another tear. I heard a voice say, "everything is going to be alright," and, "this was all meant to be." As quickly as it had begun the feeling disappeared; stunned I regained my composure and rejoined my family, telling no one of what I had just experienced. Kirby and I always had a friendship that went beyond just being cousins. We had a spiritual bond as well, though I didn't realize it until many years later. So from the time of Kirby's death in October 1981 to June of 1992 my life was an empty hole, made worse by the agonizing question of what happened on the night of the accident.

There were four different possibilities from what I can remember: the driver fell asleep; the driver had been drinking; because the driver had three separate breaks in his right arm caused by the crash, he could have been adjusting something on the dashboard control panel; or they had been run off the road. Rumor had it that Kirby and his two classmates were doing well with the local girls at the high school football game they attended and the local boys did not like it.

Whichever of these explanations proved to be true, it would be a long time before I got my answer. A third passenger sleeping in the back seat of the car survived the crash, but he had no memories from that night. So for the next eleven years I protected myself from feeling the pain of another loss by not getting too close to anyone. That changed in June of 1992, when I met my first wife. For the first time since Kirby's death I was truly happy. She was from North Devon in England, and she and I shared a spiritual bond every bit as close as Kirby and I did, and I fell so hard in love with her that when she left me over four years later, it was every bit as painful as when Kirby died, because she was the love of my life. But destiny would have different paths for us. So here I am, stuck with a double whammy of pain because of another deeply felt loss and now believing I will be alone for the rest of my life. True love only happens once in a lifetime, right? But then in May of 2001, lightning struck again when I met my current wife Shannon, and as fate would have it I was given another true love. It was Friday night on Memorial Day weekend at the Boomtown Casino and Hotel west of Reno Nevada, which by the way is a great place to stay. So here I was in the cabaret with friends watching my cousin Robert and his band, *The California Cowboys,* perform, a great band if I say so myself. Great hotel and casino, great music ... what could be more carefree and fun?

My future wife Shannon was at the other end of the casino gambling, repeatedly harassed by a very determined spirit tugging her blouse from behind and whispering in her ear, urging her to "go to the cabaret." You see my future bride to be is a psychic medium, both talented and perceptive. Shannon ignored these repeated interruptions, continuing to gamble without realizing she was about to hit a jackpot of a very different sort, one of love which is, of course, the biggest gamble of all. After about an hour and a half Shannon gave in and wandered into the cabaret, catching the last song. Standing at the table of band memorabilia, she was approached by Robert about purchasing his CDs; my cousin says, at first, "you should meet my brother Allen." Robert then changed his mind, excitedly grabbing Shannon by the arms and said, "Oh my God! You *have* to meet my cousin Bryon!" He walked Shannon over to my table and introduced her to me; we bonded immediately. We spent the entire three day weekend together and although impetuous, we knew it was meant to be.

Almost immediately, I could tell that Shannon was a very spiritual person, but I had no idea the depths of her spirituality or that she was a psychic medium. Following a whirlwind summer, I moved her down permanently to Fremont in September. During that first summer together, Shannon's psychic medium abilities were revealed in many accurate readings given to various people, strangers we would meet over the summer and during our first three years together. Just six weeks after we met, Shannon told me about the spirit who was responsible for her coming to the cabaret at Boomtown. She psychically knew this spirit was connected to me, describing this spirit as a teenage male cousin with sandy colored hair and an infectious laugh, not related by blood or marriage. Kirby was adopted, something Shannon was unaware of, and there were no photos of Kirby out for Shannon to see.

Shannon sketched out a drawing of the young man in spirit, and I immediately recognized the individual. Wanting to be sure, I grabbed a photo of Kirby out of a box in the closet and held it next to her drawing. The sketch and the photograph were nearly identical, the only difference being the length of hair: Shannon's drawing showed a young man with long hair, although Kirby's hair never went past medium length. I pointed this out to Shannon, but she merely smiled and said, "Kirby always wanted to wear his hair long and now he gets to appear however he wants." I knew this to be true. I was pretty excited because Shannon had been very accurate on everything she'd picked up about Kirby.

Over the following months, Kirby came through to Shannon a few times, but for some reason I never could get any straight answers to my questions about the night of the accident. Shannon reported that communicating with spirits is like playing charades, coming through visions, feelings, and spoken words but still very complicated and hard to explain, because there's more to it than her natural five senses. I couldn't hide my frustration. I had watched Shannon provide accurate readings for many strangers without any problems, yet as close as we were I couldn't seem to connect with the one person from whom I wanted answers. And events soon took a different course for us, away from the psychic adventures we'd enjoyed during those first three years together. Shannon's poor health took precedence, taxing us emotionally and financially as time went by.

Our lives became a constant see-saw. Shannon's ongoing health problems—which included three more surgeries and myoblocks every six months—challenged us in significant ways. It was only thanks to my family's love and support that we were able to stay out of bankruptcy during those years of struggle. Then on October 9th 2007, twenty six years after Kirby's death, Shannon and I were given a gift. And this was no ordinary gift. This was Kirby's gift.

Life is not about getting what we want.

Life is about learning from what we get.

Bryon Richard Smith

Chapter Two

The Other Side of Tomorrow

October 9, 2007, started out just like any other day. Nothing out of the ordinary happened throughout the day until about 10:20 pm when something life-altering occurred, something triggering the event that was about to unfold, though I had no idea at the time. As Shannon and I sat there in our bedroom, I noticed a smile on her face, a rare, maybe magical expression, or in this case something paranormal.

Shannon looked at me and said, "You are not going to believe this, but Kirby just showed up." I was dumbfounded.

Shannon continued: "Kirby, he's here."

Now Shannon had revealed Kirby's "pop over rights," but she quickly informed me this was different, this was something special. This time, Kirby was channeling through her, allowing him to communicate more effectively than in normal situations. If "popping over" can be considered a normal situation!

Shocked, I responded with a cocky, "Well, what does he want?"

And through Shannon, Kirby answered: "I am here and I can now answer your questions." So the first of many surprises of the night had begun. Part of the night's experience took the format of Kirby channeling through Shannon, answering questions posed by me. Situations like this one can be confusing, both for the participants and for those hearing about the experience. Understanding that Kirby speaks through Shannon, I relate the conversation we shared without referencing Shannon except when it is Shannon herself speaking.

The first *series* of questions I posed covered the repeated interventions in my life during near death experiences, but my *very* first question should be pretty obvious—what happened on the night of the accident? Kirby's answer was easy to understand: he was a typical dumb teenager, drinking and then trusting someone else who also had been drinking to drive home. He acted with a teenager's belief that he was indestructible and would live forever. Kirby warned me to never trust anyone to drive me home, which I thought sounded a little cryptic. On the night of the accident, Kirby was sitting in the front passenger seat, half-asleep and watching the headlights from the opposite side of the road pass by, when the car drifted off the road into the guardrail end cap. His friend, the driver, had fallen asleep at the wheel, and it happened so quickly he was not only completely unaware of it, but found the experience very peaceful in a strange sort of way.

His next realization was of lying in a hospital bed, surrounded by souls waiting to help guide him as he crossed over.

A soul is what exists in a physical body and is the essence of us within the Ethereal Realm—Heaven, the afterlife, or spirit world—but earthbound souls are what are known as spirits. He was also aware that the rest of his family and I were at the hospital as well. When Kirby left his body, the other souls told him I had run off on my own. It was then I was told by Kirby that it was him who came to me in the hospital chapel, not God. The information shocked me, because for twenty-six years I believed I had had a divine experience with God. Part of me felt very disappointed, but at the same time I began to feel a burden lift off of me, knowing the details of the night of the accident and that Kirby was okay in the afterlife.

The message conveyed healing and closure for me, and it seemed as if Kirby's message had been delivered. Based on other readings I'd witnessed, it would be a logical place for the session to end. Instead, the session took an unexpected and thrilling turn. Kirby would remain with Shannon and I for a while longer—a rare event—allowing me to ask him additional questions. This was the start of a lengthy session, keeping us up until after 3:30 in the morning. So I took a deep breath and began to fire off a series of questions. Unfortunately, I was completely caught off guard by all of this and I did not have time to formulate a series of predetermined questions, so I just proceeded with what I could think of on the spot. I limited my questions about the Bible, because even in an expanded session (and I had no idea how long this would continue) there was so much to probe! I was so curious about where Kirby was at and how he would describe it to me. First and foremost, I asked the big question: why he had to die so young. He was fated to die young, he explained, in his first physical life. The tragedy of dying young takes on a different meaning when viewed through a bigger meaning to the existence of life; reincarnation is how our physical life along with the afterlife works, because souls do not learn what they need to grow in just one physical lifetime.

Kirby then told me our souls first met at a transfer point within the Ethereal Realm, soon after his soul was given life but just before his first physical life as my cousin here on earth. This transfer point would be similar to a bus or train station, though with obvious differences. I am on my fourth life and Shannon is on her twelfth, Kirby explained. Shannon is, in fact, an older soul then either Kirby or I. As a New Soul, Kirby obtained needed guidance from me as to how to grow and transition through this life and the afterlife by making some ultimate form of self-sacrifice.

Every soul needs to do this in order to grow within their current level of existence or to transition to another. Kirby revealed that I had sacrificed my first physical life centuries ago in a small village made up of primitive little huts, an interesting tidbit but I didn't really care to spend more time on it. Of greater interest to me was the message that Shannon and I have been together in some of our prior lives in different incarnations. In one life, for example, we were brothers; in another, we were married but each as the opposite gender. The same held true regarding our former spouses. Apparently, Shannon and I have known our former spouses in past lives. And as for future lives, we're destined to travel that road with each other and with those former spouses. Spending time with a particular soul helps them grow in those areas they need to develop, and they help you grow as well. These lessons can be positive or they can be negative, but they are all a means for us to gain knowledge for our own personal growth, allowing us each to fulfill our own destiny.

I felt compelled to ask Kirby why my first wife left me (which was a little uncomfortable due to the fact that Kirby was channeling through my current wife, but I had to know to achieve complete closure; plus I knew Shannon is a very understanding woman and this would not be an issue for her). The answer Kirby gave me will remain private, but suffice to say that answer helped me to understand why she left. I wish her well and hope she finds happiness in this life. I also asked about the driver of Kirby's car on the night of the accident—Kirby revealed that he had been reborn into the physical world almost immediately after his death. All intriguing questions and the answers were fascinating, but now I moved on to issues involving my own spiritual experiences.

In particular, I had questions about several near death experiences that began shortly after Kirby's death and continued throughout my life. I'd felt a guardian angel watching over me and Kirby confirmed that he had intervened several times on my behalf. In fact, had Kirby lived, I would have died young instead, but not before I would have had children of my own. It was an interesting alternative life: I had chosen *not* to have children because of the pain of possibly losing one, a fear directly related to the pain I felt at Kirby's death. I don't handle loss very well at all, carrying the loss of a loved one with me as though there is no end in sight. This even applies to pets.

My first near death experience occurred on my 18th birthday, two weeks after Kirby's death. I was still in the depths of grief, coping by drinking so much alcohol that I passed out, slowly dying of alcohol poisoning. In this subconscious death wish, I would have been successful to if not for Kirby. In what can only be described as a graphically gross intervention, Kirby stuck his ghost finger half way down my throat to get my gag reflex going, causing me to vomit the alcohol I had consumed. About a year later I once again came close to dying, this time from a car collision that would have been my fault. I was behind the wheel, driving while adjusting the stereo and I failed to notice stopped traffic ahead of me on the freeway. Something warned me to look up from the stereo, simultaneously slamming on my brakes and swerving to miss the stopped cars. I skidded three full car lengths on the shoulder between the center divider and the fast lane. I immediately thought of Kirby and felt he had warned me about the impending collision.

But my third near death experience seemed the most symbolic. A year later I was driving from Albuquerque, New Mexico to Fremont, California on highway 40; about two hours east of Winslow, Arizona I fell asleep at the wheel of my Datsun 280z. Dirt and gravel kicked up against the undercarriage of my car as I drifted off the highway, waking me up suddenly, like a splash of cold water on my face. I immediately slammed on the brakes and went into several spins before coming to a stop about twenty feet from a guardrail end cap, the same kind of guardrail end cap that took Kirby's life. I was so scared and so angry that I started to cuss myself out, until I realized the significance of the moment. I knew Kirby had watched over me again, so I quietly thanked him for my life. Other incidents followed, all in a similar vein. But for whatever reasons I have been blessed with spiritual protection, including a spirit guide by the name of Brenda Ann. According to Kirby, she was my sister in a prior life who has intervened in my later near death experiences. Kirby then told me to never call her Raggedy Ann because that is not her real name and she hates that, and while this information is a little quirky, it is informative with regards to what was said during the reading. From this point on, my questions changed direction. Rather than focus on me, I began to probe the nature of the afterlife in general, along with questions on various other subjects. The answers Kirby provided profoundly changed Shannon and I forever, answers that may just change you forever too.

There is no such thing as a final resting place.

I will come back and I will be better than before.

The only sadness in that is you will not know it's me.

And neither will I.

Bryon Richard Smith

Chapter Three

The Ethereal Realm and Hell

My faith growing up was based on the Christian beliefs taught in church and in our home. I still consider myself a Christian, though far more spiritual then religious. Perhaps it's because I've never been satisfied relying on what other people think or teach or write about. I wanted first-hand knowledge, truth without someone else's religion, politics, or point of view influencing the information. Especially following Kirby's death, I wanted answers, and I wanted those answers to come from a pure source, away from the influence of anyone here on earth. Power, money, and ideology work to convince or corrupt people into believing just about anything. It's one reason why I believe in Kirby's words. He stands to gain nothing by all of this, unless it's to affirm an outlook about God, the Afterlife, and our purpose in the universe in a healing manner. Especially for those lacking faith or who have become discouraged with religion in general, Kirby's message is a reassuring reflection on life's meaning, particularly upon the loss of a loved one. Significantly, his message is offered to bring healing and understanding to people in the confusion and pain that comes with loss. With that being said then let's begin.

∞

I now asked Kirby, "What is the Afterlife like?"

His response took the shape of a detailed map outlining the experience of passing from this life to another. He explained that the afterlife is an Ethereal Realm existing not within the confines of our universe or dimension, but that exists within a time and place outside of our comprehension. The closest way for us to understand it is to consider a sphere within a sphere within a sphere, creating layer upon layer upon layer. Existence is structured within these layers of time, matter, space, energy, destiny, and dimensions, they are all as one yet separate within their own layer, it is eternal with no beginning and no end. Although existence is not completely limited to time, matter, space, energy, destiny, or dimensions in any way shape or form, it is similarly structured as such. As a soul passes from the physical world into the Ethereal Realm, the sensation of a body continues, although obviously that connection has been severed. An initial feeling of weightlessness changes, as the soul becomes grounded within the Ethereal Realm. In short, the soul lacks tangible weight such as a body experiences, resulting in the feeling of weightlessness, but without actually floating around.

All the burdens of one's physical life fade away as the soul slips into a peaceful calm. But the senses, or a representation of the senses we identify, send a flurry of data. Visually, a bluish white light and undefined shadowy images appear within a cloudy veil, evoking a familiarity that helps the soul transition into the Ethereal Realm. Voices are also heard, coming from all directions as if in a crowded room, but the voices will be very peaceful. There is no smell and there is no sensation of breathing. You will have a sense of energy around you and it will feel like tingles from static electricity. Your soul's energy will at this point still project itself into a bodily shape, but without physical mass.

Some souls are able to cross back and forth between the physical world and the Ethereal Realm, projecting an appearance into whatever form is desired, usually choosing a form that others will recognize. The longer you are there the more defined everything will become, but the passage of time is perceived very differently than it is in the physical world. When a soul passes over, others are there to greet them, though not necessarily people from the life immediately completed. These are friends and family from many prior lives who welcome the soul home and reconnect us to our ethereal soul.

The type of soul passing over dictates the length of time spent interacting with the soul's comrades during the pre-transition. Pre-transition is time spent prior to a subsequent life, whether it is physical or ethereal. For some this may mean spending time experiencing moments missed while living their physical life. For example, they may have suffered limitations out of their control while on earth, but are now able to fulfill what was lacking and prepare themselves for another physical life. Or the soul may learn from missed experiences due to a premature death in the most recent physical life. For others this is a time of reflection and planning for the next physical life they choose to have. While some souls have no choice and will begin a new physical life right away, there are many variables involved with pre-transition. As for the layout of the Ethereal Realm immediately after we cross over to it would be similar to being in a complex with a series of levels and pathways that are part of a transfer point that leads further into the Ethereal Realm.

This initial area is structured much like the physical world, but without its confines and none of its limitations. The familiarity of the initial entry point of the Ethereal Realm with the physical world is to help you cross over into it with more ease. This transfer point is also the area that functions like a bus or train station. You all know the Ethereal Realm exists, not out of a need to believe in something more but from recessed memories from before your physical life began. How you access these memories depends on a variety of things: where you were born, how you were raised, the inner workings of your particular religion, your cultural impressions, and whether previous near death experiences or contact with a Guardian Soul have left you especially sensitive.

In terms of concrete imagery, Kirby showed Shannon only what lies just beyond the physical world. Beyond this transitional area, there is much more to experience; the Ethereal Realm is certainly not limited to what Kirby was able to transmit to Shannon. While Shannon gained only a glimpse of what exists within the Ethereal Realm, she *was* given extensive knowledge on how and why it works. Psychic perception, visions, emotional feelings, and Kirby's own words came together and channeled through Shannon, enabling her to better communicate with me and then with others through the writing of this book. One noteworthy point: since Shannon's soul did not leave her body, she did not experience the tunnel effect found with people who go through near death experiences, nor did her soul move into either the pre-transition state or the Ethereal Realm.

∞

I next asked Kirby, "Is there a Hell?"

Personally I never believed in Hell, but I still felt compelled to ask this question. Kirby's response was complex, but understandable.

The short answer to my inquiry was that there is no hell in the traditional religious sense, but you do create your own hell by how you live, how you treat others, and how you learn from your choices. Your current life will affect what kind of a life you will have in the next, whether it is physical or ethereal. The key, Kirby emphasized, was improving upon yourself. If you fail to learn from your mistakes and your shortcomings, you will be doomed to repeat the process until you have changed your ways.

Living for others is also key. As human beings, we need to make some ultimate form of self-sacrifice that is highly personalized and will help an individual, group, or situation in order to transition into another type of soul. But it needs to be completely sincere and selfless on your part, not undertaken out of obligation or resentment. It also does not need to be a well thought out action, it can be something completely reactionary like spontaneously saving someone from impending danger. Even defending an underdog from bullying or nursing someone who's ill constitutes service for your fellow human beings.

But this sacrifice can take on many different incarnations. Selfish persons, or individuals who fail to sincerely sacrifice for others, or those who do not learn from their mistakes will remain as Revolving Souls. Revolving Souls are continually reborn into subsequent lives with ongoing hardships, but still pose similar opportunities to grow within your current level or transition into a another one.

Ultimately your faith is your belief in a higher power.

How you practice it is up to you and not by anyone else

here on earth.

Bryon Richard Smith

Chapter Four

Matters of Religion

My next round of questions focused on God and the Bible, but not about obscure passages or tricky doctrinal issues or even the obvious ones. In the little time I had with Kirby, I wanted to know more about his perspective on the afterlife. And frankly, I was just happy to be talking with him again. I avoided the basic "is there a God"—because I always believed in God. The complexities of the universe seemed like proof in and of itself of an intelligent design by a Supreme Being. Because if there was no Supreme Being, would I be talking to my dead cousin? Would there be an afterlife without a God? I was less concerned about God's existence than God's character.

So I then asked Kirby, "What is God Like?"

God is known as the *Original Soul* within the Ethereal Realm, with both male and female aspects. These aspects are not physical in nature and are more associated with the internal mysteries of the ethereal soul. God always has been and always will be and isn't defined in a traditional human religious context. The physical world limits our ability to define or fully understand the Original Soul. Although the Original Soul refrains from direct involvement with individual lives, it's clear that humans are not alone. Destiny is the essence of the Original Soul's knowledge, an entity unto itself that aids souls on their journeys for growth and enlightenment, both in the physical and the ethereal states of being. A grand design commands and controls the physical world and the Ethereal Realm, with destiny playing a key role in that design. Guardian and Guiding Souls are responsible for these duties as well. The Original Soul enabled the forces for the universe to be created, allowing physical life to exist.

∞

I am not exactly trusting of human nature. I see the ways in which people use, manipulate, and distort all religions to fit their personal agendas, be it for good or evil. Anything written by a human being is easily influenced by the self-interests of the author. What purpose could be served by asking Kirby questions about disputed passages from the Bible? My focus, then, settled on areas of interest to me.

So I asked Kirby, "Were The Ten Commandments actually written by the Hand of God?"

His answer intrigued me. The Ten Commandments are the only earthly laws provided by the Original Soul. Beyond these laws, individual souls are free to succeed or fail according to their actions and choices, allowing our souls to grow from those choices and the consequences that follow. And while our souls possess the freedom to choose our own path, we are unable to grow beyond the limits placed upon us by destiny. Each individual must look within themselves to learn and grow and to do what is right without outside influences. When extensive rules govern our thoughts and actions, we lose the ability to learn from our inherent knowledge of good and evil, a knowledge created within each soul from the time we are given life. How we choose to use that knowledge is the truest test of our ethereal soul.

∞

I asked Kirby, "Was Jesus a Real Person?"

To traditional religion, this question might seem like blasphemy. But the answer I received was so intriguing, I'm glad I asked it.

Jesus, Kirby explained, was a real, but very powerful Guiding Soul, one of the most powerful Guiding Souls that ever walked the earth. Although Jesus was a child of the Original Soul, he was conceived, born, and raised in the same manner as other human beings. Jesus came to earth for a specific purpose: to help mankind rise up out of a very dark time in human history. As a uniquely evolved Guiding Soul, Jesus was not completely limited by destiny. Particularly powerful is the fact that destiny could not confine Jesus within its normal boundaries, meaning that Jesus controlled his fate to a much greater degree than other human beings. Nonetheless, Jesus chose to follow his fate through to finality.

Jesus was also not the only *Living Guiding Soul* placed on earth to enlighten mankind. The Original Soul sent Guiding Souls to every other religion, to bring wisdom and guidance to all humanity. Indeed, the initial purpose of the Original Soul's teachings for the human race—before and after the Guiding Souls such as Jesus—was to provide positive healing, guidance, and understanding for all. But mankind corrupted religion by co-opting it exclusively into native cultures, and by writing it strictly from a man's perspective. Religion was overly edited by man, for man, and to empower man.

Another example of this is not only writings within all religions but also the writings of Jesus' miracles there in the physical world which was greatly exaggerated. The true miracle of Jesus and the other Guiding Souls is not what was written about their earthly miracles but more about their message of a Supreme Being and life after death because our true existence is as an ethereal soul and not the bodies that we inhabit there in the physical world. Physical bodies are just tools to help us learn and grow in the physical world so these lessons can be carried back into the Ethereal Realm.

∞

This next question is not about the Bible, but it is going to be just as controversial. I have always felt that abortion is morally wrong, but from a legal perspective I support a woman's right to choose. As a man I always felt it was incredibly arrogant for any man to tell a woman what she can or cannot do with her own body, especially here in America where we hold freedom dear above all else. But my own personal hope is that women will choose life over death without some government telling them they can or cannot do so. And for the record Shannon is pro-choice, but now she is not so sure.

Realizing that abortion is a hot topic issue that creates strong passions, I now asked Kirby, "When does Life Begin?"

Physical life begins at the first moment of conception. Souls are drawn to the sexual energy of human beings, so that when a couple is making love, although the woman may or may not conceive, a soul will be drawn from the Ethereal Realm to the couple's location in the physical world. The soul can enter the woman's body and the fetus at the very first moment of biological conception. All living physical beings require a soul in order to generate a life force that is the power within that soul. The mother can only supply physical needs to the fetus for a short time, so in order for the fetus to stay viable, a soul is required to exist within it. This explains why some fetuses miscarry on their own for no apparent medical reason. Essentially, a soul with freedom of choice may decide to enter the fetus, or to leave and wait for another physical life.

It's not unusual for a soul to choose the destination for its physical life according to its life purpose, even if that purpose is short-lived. For example, to grow within your current level or to transition into another, a soul may choose a life that will be aborted or die prematurely, or born with mental or physical challenges. These are self-sacrificing acts that open up opportunities to the lives they touch, or to guide and teach another soul that is currently living in the physical world.

The meaning of life for each is as individual

as there are souls.

Shannon Amy Smith

Chapter Five

Broader Questions

With all of the interest and speculation about life on other planets I had to ask Kirby this next question:

"Is there life elsewhere in the universe?"

Life, according to Kirby, is everywhere, not only in this universe but in others as well. Life exists in other dimensions too, and they all resemble the human beings inhabiting earth. For ethereal reasons, the human race is not supposed to know of these other lives, which is why extraterrestrial life appears non-human in earthly sightings. Those alien designs so popular are strictly the product of Hollywood fantasy or scientific speculation. The similarity between humans and the beings living on other planets or in other dimensions extends beyond physical appearance. All planets, galaxies, universes, timelines, and dimensions that make up existence are part of the Ethereal Realm and are on the same journey of growth and learning.

Souls reborn into their next physical life usually travel to the same planet they inhabited in prior lives, but there are exceptions. A soul—or souls—can be reborn elsewhere, as when a planet is destroyed and an entire civilization vanishes. For the most part, though, we are drawn back to what we know and understand, with the majority of souls reincarnating to familiar places in the physical world. Remember: the Original Soul's creation of existence is incomprehensible for a soul in the physical world.

∞

Since Kirby died, I've experienced a handful of dreams in which Kirby and I are together again. These dreams feel metaphysical, not as in a memory of past events. I am fully aware that Kirby has died even as I dream, and I recognize that Kirby is visiting from the afterlife. And so it was natural for me to ask Kirby, "Are dreams another way of communicating with people who have crossed over?"

Most dreams involving a loved one who has died are strictly from the subconscious mind, but there are times when a soul uses the dream state to either transmit a message or to simply visit, wishing to convey to a loved one that they are loved and remembered. Dreams are a natural and easier way for some souls to communicate. The challenge, of course, comes in determining whether a particular dream is metaphysical or from the subconscious. It was reassuring to hear that Kirby had, in actuality, visited me through my dreams.

Living Beyond Existence

∞

As a teenager in the late 1970s, I saw a documentary film that explored the mysteries of life and death. One segment focused on weighing animals at the moment of death, to determine whether they lost even a fractional weight as the soul would have escaped the body. According to the scientists, there was no change in weight. The same experiment performed on a terminally ill human volunteer revealed that the man lost about one pound at the moment of death. It was speculated the one pound loss was the soul leaving the body. I do not remember the name of the documentary, but I've never forgotten that particular experiment.

And so I asked Kirby, "Do animals have souls?"

In fact, animals do have souls. Animals are nonhuman souls, limited in intelligence but with roughly the same range of emotions that human souls possess. All living physical beings require a soul in order to generate a life force that is the power within that soul, regardless of whether that soul is human or not. Animal souls are the only nonhuman souls that exist and they cannot transition into a human soul. Their very existence is to be continually reborn into the physical world because this is their destiny.

∞

In recent years, there have been a lot of 2012 doomsday predictions. Back as far as early 2007 certain cable TV channels began airing shows predicting the destruction of the world and life as we know it. It's a troubling scenario, to say the least.

I now asked Kirby, "Will the human race and/or earth be destroyed in 2012?"

I almost thought I heard Kirby laugh. Mankind has tried to predict the end of the world almost as long as it has existed, and 2012 is yet one more example. Change happens, and Earth will experience some major and some minor changes, but all the doomsday paranoia is exactly that, paranoia. That isn't to say earth will last forever, but its day of destruction lies in the distant future.

∞

I now asked Kirby, "Does Bigfoot really exist?"

Kirby responds; What?

I'm actually kidding. There's no way I would have asked Kirby that kind of a question. I just had to get a little bit of my sense of humor into this book.

Self sacrifice is not only the best way to help others.

It is also the best way to help ourselves grow.

Bryon Richard Smith

Chapter Six

The Souls of Existence

THE ORIGINAL SOUL (God/Supreme Being)

The concept of the Original Soul often baffles the human mind, because human beings live in a finite world with definite limitations of time and space. In fact, the Original Soul is an ethereal being that incorporates both male and female aspects, but is neither exclusively. The Original Soul enabled all forces to create the universe, all that exist there, everywhere and for all time. While caring for each and every being, the Original Soul does not intervene in individual lives. Our lives are filled with good and with bad, and consequences that derive from both our own freedom of choice and from the power of destiny. The Original Soul established the grand design commanding and controlling our existence, both on the physical plane and in the Ethereal Realm. Within that design, souls pursue their journey with the assistance of Guardian and Guiding Souls, in conjunction with destiny. The Original Soul does not think of itself as a God as we use the term in the physical world.

ETERNAL SOULS (Elders)

Eternal Souls co-exist with the Original Soul in the Ethereal Realm, having lived a great many physical and ethereal lives. For some, this would equate to a belief in Heaven and or retirement from the physical world. Due to their age and their openness to learn, Eternal Souls have great wisdom and valuable experience. Souls do not exist in a static state, however, and at any time a soul may choose to inhabit another life in the physical world, even after existing within the Ethereal Realm for extended periods of time.

GUARDIAN SOULS (Guardian/Warrior Angels)

Guardian Souls have earned their position through some ultimate form of self sacrifice in the physical world and act as both guardians and warriors. While these entities serve as guardians for all souls, some are specifically assigned to protect Gifted Souls from the Dark Souls, which are drawn to the energy of Gifted Souls in both ethereal but especially in physical form. Guardian Souls are very powerful and have the ability to alter destiny in limited ways, moving between the Ethereal Realm and the physical world at will. As warriors, Guardian Souls alone possess powers that can be used offensively or defensively.

Throughout time there has been an ongoing battle between Guardian Souls and Dark Souls.

GUIDING SOULS (Spirit Guides)

Guiding Souls help other souls as they navigate their journey in the physical realm, often steering Gifted Souls along the right path. Guiding Souls have what Shannon calls "pop over rights," allowing them to travel between the Ethereal Realm and the physical world at will. Guiding Souls would be considered teachers within the Ethereal Realm. On a limited basis, Guiding Souls may perform limited Guardian Soul duties, but their intervention is limited to those situations where a life is at stake and the Guardian Soul can assist in saving the life. Guiding Souls enjoy a symbiotic relationship with Gifted Souls that is unique within the Souls of Existence.

GIFTED SOULS (Psychics/Mediums)

Gifted Souls spend many lifetimes in the physical world as powerful sensitives. The specific destiny of Gifted Souls is to help other souls find their way. Psychic mediums reveal elements of the future by tapping into the complex subtleties of destiny, communicating with souls that have crossed over but are here as either earthbound spirits or souls that have crossed over into the Ethereal Realm. Gifted

Souls predominantly communicate with Guiding Souls, Lost Souls, or Dark Souls, but the interaction is not limited to those three types of souls. Gifted Souls have a symbiotic relationship with Guiding Souls that is unique within the Souls of Existence.

TIMELESS SOULS (Watchers)

Timeless Souls opt to pursue lives within the Ethereal Realm in a manner comparable to a physical life, because they prefer the Ethereal Realm over the physical world. This choice is possible due to wisdom gained and sacrifices made during their physical lives, but Timeless Souls must still occasionally live out a physical life from time to time. At this level, a soul's existence will fundamentally shift into a more ethereal state of being, since greater knowledge is shown at this level about the Ethereal Realm and life within it.

TRANSIT SOULS (Planners)

Transit Souls communicate with one another within the Ethereal Realm's transfer point, utilizing their freedom of choice—earned through personal growth and sacrifices—to decide the type of physical life to assume next. With their detailed strategic planning and insight, Transit Souls are a key component to the grand design of existence. At this level, a soul becomes more aware of transitioning within existence and chooses in broad terms their next physical life. Transit Souls also communicate with New Souls, those souls replacing an existing soul lost to a Dark Soul, guiding them in planning their physical life.

PHYSICAL SOULS (Seekers)

Physical Souls enjoy living in the physical world, so they spend more time there than in the Ethereal Realm. Physical Souls are comparable to worker bees, keeping everything in motion. The physical world could not function without this type of soul. Upon death, these souls are drawn back to the physical world even though they have no choice in the type of life they will experience. Practical and pragmatic, Physical Souls believe in varying degrees that if they can't see it, touch it, or smell it, then it probably doesn't exist. They are also people who live their physical lives as if it's their only one, because they truly believe only in the here and now. Along with Revolving Souls, Physical Souls provide the most numerous types of souls.

REVOLVING SOULS (Instant Repeaters)

Revolving Souls are instantly returned to the physical world as soon as they arrive in the Ethereal Realm. Instant reincarnation allows them to relearn the lessons missed during previous stints in the physical world. These individuals do not learn from negative emotions and struggle with the importance of humility and forgiveness. Always quick to provide an excuse for their behavior and their choices, Revolving Souls frequently fail to learn from their own failures and mistakes. These souls are sent back to the physical world as they struggle to find their true purpose in their physical life. Revolving souls are still under the direct control by the Original Soul's power over destiny, without a choice as to the type of life they will find on the physical plane. As with Physical Souls, Revolving Souls are among the most common types of soul existing in the physical world.

LOST SOULS (Ghosts)

Lost Souls become caught between the physical world and the Ethereal Realm, struggling to return to the physical world without moving deeper into the Ethereal Realm. The urge to remain in the physical world comes from one of two motivations: either a life goal remains incomplete, or they retain a longing desire to communicate with the physical world, whether for positive or negative reasons. Rarely, a Lost Soul may be salvaged through the guidance of a Gifted Soul, who helps the Lost Soul transition into another soul. Physical, Revolving, Insane,

Hungry, Dark and New Souls are most susceptible to becoming Lost Souls.

INSANE SOULS (Hell/Purgatory)

Insane Souls live out physical and ethereal lives that are incapable of accepting the concept of crossing over between the physical world and the Ethereal Realm. Often these souls embrace extremely rigid belief systems that confuse and damage souls, so they are unable to advance or find peace to maintain their sanity. This form of hell relates not to an individual's evil character or as punishment for evil acts, but rather reflects insanity on the part of the soul. In other words, the soul creates this hell within itself. Not all Insane Souls are doomed for eternity. Interventions from other souls may open up opportunities, allowing Insane Souls to find their path and regain their sanity, opening up the opportunity to transition into another type of soul. Physical, Revolving, Lost, and New Souls are most susceptible to becoming Insane Souls.

HUNGRY SOULS (Power Hungry Villains/Leaders)

Hungry Souls are able to use subliminal memories from their ethereal life to an advantage in their physical life, in particular in the pursuit of power. Their hunger for power is insatiable, and these souls tend to manipulate Dark

Souls. Hungry Souls enjoy creating chaos by stirring up emotions in Dark Souls. Hungry Souls can be powers for either positive or negative goals, but their deceptive nature leads more often to negative goals. Certain powerful authority figures, whether villains or leaders, fall into this category of soul.

DARK SOULS (Demons)

Dark Souls, when in the physical world, are bad, cruel, or evil people who may or may not feel remorse for their actions. If caught between the physical world and the Ethereal Realm, these demonic entities have the power to seek out and harm all souls but especially Gifted Souls. They are human entities and are the henchmen of the Hungry Souls, yet they fail to recognize the manipulation practiced by Hungry Souls. If a Dark Soul finds true redemption, it faces the opportunity to be reborn into the physical world as an innocent, starting on a new life path. Dark Souls and Guardian Souls engage in an ongoing battle, as they have done throughout time.

NEW SOULS (Newbie's)

As indicated by their name, New Souls have recently been given life or are still on their first physical life. They are rare and celebrated within the Ethereal Realm, but unfortunately the event is preceded by the loss of an existing soul to a Dark Soul. The loss is usually a Gifted Soul that has succumbed to a Dark Soul, though it can happen to any type of soul. In general, the number of souls in existence remains constant because the current number of souls is sufficient to live out infinite lives in infinite places in infinite combinations. But if and when that balance changes, it comes from the Original Soul through the power of destiny. Embarking on a new life journey, the New Soul doesn't necessarily act with limited knowledge and experience. Sometimes a New Soul gains the advantage of an existing soul's insights and experience due to an early sacrifice in their first physical life or because they are a needed replacement for an existing soul that has been lost to a Dark Soul. Hence Kirby became one of Shannon's spirit guides (Guiding Soul), despite the fact he is still considered a New Soul.

ANIMAL SOULS (Nonhuman)

Animal Souls are the only souls that are nonhuman in nature. They are always returned to the physical world after crossing into the Ethereal Realm, unless they have formed a very close connection with a human soul as their pet. In those cases, the Animal Soul is allowed to remain for a limited time within the Ethereal Realm, but ultimately must return to the physical world. Animal Souls may be limited in intelligence, but they basically experience roughly the same range of emotions possessed by human souls. All living physical beings whether human or not require a soul in order to generate a life force that is the power within that soul. Animal Souls cannot advance to a human level soul.

ADDITIONAL INFO

Despite popular belief, there is no Devil, or Satan, or Lucifer. That character simply does not exist. Likewise, inhuman demonic entities are a concept of human beings rather than a reality and do not exist, instead, demons are in actually, Dark Souls. There is no hell, except for what we create through our own choices in life, how we treat others, and by how we learn from adversity. Our willingness to sacrifice for others and our ability to learn lessons necessary for us to grow—these are ultimately the things that determine whether our next physical or ethereal life will be a living hell or a life of spiritual comfort. There is nothing dark, evil, or negative that equals or comes remotely close to challenging the Original Soul in power, strength, wisdom, intelligence, and supreme presence. We create all of the evil in this life and the afterlife because evil is limited to just us, but we can also defeat evil. This brings us to the entities known as *Shadow People*.

Shadow People are human entities that are negative or evil; they are Lost, Hungry, or Dark Souls. A Shadow

Person is not a type of soul, although it is spiritual in nature, it is merely another way for one of these existing souls to manifest itself in a more malevolent form here in the physical world.

      Whether in the physical world or the Ethereal Realm, we remain the same type of soul, although there is no way for us to know or determine what type of soul we are in the physical world, but it is only in the physical world where we are given the opportunity to change, grow, and transition through the Souls of Existence. For many, their soul gains knowledge and grows within itself without the need to transition into another soul, while others may be destined to make that transition. Regardless, it is important to recognize that many souls are content at their current level and will continue to grow within that level only. There is also no hierarchy involved within the Souls of Existence comparable to the physical world—all souls are considered equal. So our destiny may be to transition or it may not be to transition, but the challenge remains to grow in spirit, whether it is within one level or many. As we experience life within the Ethereal Realm and the physical world, the forces controlling that experience comes directly from the Original Soul's power over destiny. Destiny allows us the freedom to make our own choices, although only to a certain point. More often than not, if we lack wisdom or selflessness, our decisions will lead us down the path to trouble rather than growth and positive experiences.

Destiny does not limit our potential

Destiny gives potential to reach our limit

Bryon Richard Smith

Chapter Seven

The Year of Hell

By this time I hope you recognize the amazing gift Kirby gave Shannon and I and, vicariously, to you as well. But all gifts come with a price, and with the good also come the bad. For Shannon and I, the bad turned out to be the year of hell. Kirby revealed that the information he conveyed to us was not normally released to the physical world, and that dark forces would try to dissuade us from writing this book. But he encouraged us to proceed with this book, asserting that it would inspire many even while creating controversy, not only in the physical world but also within the Ethereal Realm. In short, the information in this book provides too much knowledge about the afterlife. Kirby's warning did not take long to rear its ugly head. The day after our communication with him, Shannon telephoned, very upset and crying about how she was having visions of her own death.

Shannon interpreted her visions as a warning that we should not write this book. I reassured her, reminding Shannon that Kirby warned us to expect negative events, whether paranormal or physical in nature. To be honest,

Shannon felt much more afraid of these consequences than I was, largely due to her psychic abilities. Boy, was I wrong! Over the course of the next year, we were nearly overwhelmed by frequent attempts to dissuade us from writing this book. These setbacks were physical rather than paranormal in origin, and I suffered severe injuries that left me disabled even as I write. Shannon was sufficiently nervous to reach out to Kirby, expressing her fear for her life. Kirby responded, telling Shannon how he was reprimanded for revealing too much about the Ethereal Realm. As a New Soul unaware that he had violated a key principle of the Ethereal Realm, the powers that be were lenient with him. Kirby reassured Shannon that she would survive these dark days and co-author this book with me, although its publication would be delayed until late 2011 or 2012.

Again, Kirby's gift came to us on October 9th and 10th of 2007, so some years have lapsed before the book was ready to launch. The second attempt to dissuade us from writing this book came some three days before Thanksgiving 2007. Following a wonderful evening of a movie, and then dinner, Shannon's throat began to itch and her breathing became labored. Shannon suffers from a deathly allergy to peanuts, and cross contamination at the restaurant was now sending her body into anaphylactic shock. Shannon immediately injected an epinephrine pen into her thigh and I drove her to the emergency room, where we spent the next three hours while she received treatment. Suffice to say Shannon survived, but she felt sick for the next two weeks.

Dealing with a peanut allergy requires constant vigilance. Shannon and I have been together since May of 2001, and in those seven years we were always very careful about informing restaurants about her allergy and insuring they did not use peanuts or peanut oil in their meals, or even if there was any chance of cross contamination. Never had anything like this happened. Coincidence? Maybe, but we believe this was a forceful attempt to interfere with our delivering the message we received from Kirby.

The third attempt came a month later during the Christmas-New Year Holidays. Shannon and I travelled to Washington State to spend the holidays with her two daughters, enjoying a nice holiday season with Shannon's family. On our last day there, we stopped at a local restaurant where Shannon had eaten numerous times over the years without any problems. Shannon again suffered a potentially fatal exposure to peanut oil, this time as an ingredient in the salad dressing. This was much more serious than cross contamination, enough to kill Shannon inside of twenty minutes. A call to 911 and two epinephrine injections to her thigh held off death; meanwhile, I got onto my knees in front of Shannon, whose throat was beginning to close up, looked her in the eyes, and calmly reminded her that she was going to be okay. This was not her time. I

reminded her that Kirby warned us bad things like this
might occur, but we would survive them. Shannon
continued to cry as her breathing became more labored. I
held her hands as we waited for the ambulance, a wait that
seemed like an eternity although the ambulance took only
five minutes to arrive. I felt a huge weight lift off of me
when I heard the siren and then saw the ambulance pull
into the parking lot.

Despite my belief in Kirby's assurances, I was scared
as hell. I watched as the paramedics took Shannon away in
the ambulance to the local hospital, but it was only later
that I learned Shannon had begun to go into respiratory
failure in the ambulance, requiring a large dose of
epinephrine via an injection to save her life. Shannon and I
spent the entire day in the emergency room, and the next
three days with her Grandmother while Shannon slowly
recovered enough to make the road trip back to California.
This peanut allergy episode kept Shannon ill for close to two
months.

And still the problems continued. In mid-March,
Shannon and I were staying at a hotel in Fresno for my
work when I slipped in the bathroom and dislocated my left
knee. Being self-employed without a steady income, we
couldn't afford health insurance; past bouts with Shannon's
health problems had wiped us out financially, and even to
this day I suffer from severe knee pain from soft tissue
damage in need of surgical repair. Instead, I wear a knee

brace, trying to keep a worse injury from occurring. I should point out that I am not a clumsy person—I grew up playing sports including basketball, baseball, and the martial arts. Also, during the 2004-2005 Celtic fair seasons I participated in a sword fighting guild called the *"Highlander Warriors,"* based out of Fremont, a great guild for mastering swordplay and for learning about Scottish and Irish history. I never suffered an injury remotely close to being this serious. After three warnings in the form of physical injuries, I finally got the point. Something out there was not happy with this project and our determination to share Kirby's message.

And it doesn't end there. In May of 2008, I learned David, a friend since 1977, died from an accidental prescription drug overdose. David slipped on ice and broke his back in mid March of 2008, around the same time I had slipped and dislocated my knee. David lived in South Dakota, so I hadn't seen him for awhile, but his wife told me David was in a back brace that ran from underneath his arms to the top of his hips. He'd been having a particularly bad day, so he took some pain medication and laid down in their bedroom to rest; when she first checked on him, about half an hour later, he was asleep. But another thirty minutes went by, she checked on him again, and this time found he was not breathing. The 911 call was made, the paramedics arrived, but David was already gone.

Crippled and in grief over my friend's death, I watched as a new physical warning appeared, again, this time to Shannon. In July of 2008, Shannon's Methicillin-Resistant Staphylococcus Aureus (MRSA) infection returned. This infection was in remission since her fifth back surgery in 2004, but now returned with a vengeance. Shannon spent ten days in the hospital's infectious disease ward as her doctors pushed her MRSA back into remission. She was extremely lucky—if not treated, MRSA is fatal. Our year from hell closed with one more tragedy. My cousin Gary was only in his mid-50s when he died on Christmas Eve from poor health. Without question, 2008 was one of the worst years of my life.

But to every dark cloud there is, as they say, a silver lining. The saving grace of 2008 came with the writing of the first chapter to this book in September. And then something astounding happened. In October of 2008, a year after Kirby's Gift, I began writing poetry rhymes out of nowhere. I never was interested in poetry. I never read any poetry. I am very ignorant of poetry. If my life depended on it, I couldn't have rhymed *Joe* and *blow*! But something moved me to write, and to write poetry rhymes in particular. Between October, 2008, and January, 2009, I wrote 66 poems for my first book. Shannon has been writing off and on most of her adult life, so I added 10 of her poems and created the manuscript *Poems from Purgatory*. In November, 2008, the manuscript was accepted for a first volume of poetry; through October, 2011, I have seven books of poetry. *The Purgatory Series* includes *Poems from Purgatory, Poems for Your Pleasure, Poems of Perception, Poems of Perfection, Poems of Persuasion, Poems that are Preferred,* and *Poems in No Particular Order.* Each book contains between 66 and 82 of my poems.

Each volume includes a number of spiritual poems that are heavily influenced by Kirby's channeling through Shannon. The first two purgatory books highlight Shannon's poems within their pages as well. Originally I planned to release one book a year, but my publication plans are changing; with the idea of releasing a boxed set after this book is released. Only time will tell what will happen. I have also started writing a science fiction story titled *The Destiny Trilogy* as well as a series of children's books titled *Trolley the Tarantula* and I have envisioned a new trilogy titled *The Paranormals*, which centers on teenage psychics. All of these projects were conceived in the month of October, 2009. Future projects include *The Ethereals,* which came to me in October 2010, and *The Moaning Diaries,* which came to me in October 2011. I plan to have all of these published. I can't say if it means anything, but Kirby was born in April and my nightmare of the accident was in April; I was born in October, Kirby died in October, the reading with Kirby was in October, and a year later in October I began to write poetry. Each October that followed, I began conceiving more and more stories. Coincidence? Maybe, but I believe all of these poems and stories I am now writing is inspired from a greater power. Is it yet another gift from Kirby? Considering that writing poetry and becoming a writer had never crossed my mind before, due to no interest, no talent, and no writing ability of any kind, then yeah, I would have to answer yes to that one.

Tears are the pain of the soul growing.

Happiness that follows is the soul healed.

Shannon Amy Smith

Chapter Eight

Journey's End

By now some of you might think Shannon and I are
nothing more than nut jobs, in need of a nice padded cell.
In all honesty, I would probably be thinking the same thing
if I were in your place. I'm a very skeptical person when it
comes to claims made by other people, but I am open to the
possibility of finding truth in the oddest of places. So I can
only reassure you that we are not crazy, none of this account
is imagined, and what we are sharing is absolutely true!
Some will also say Shannon invented the interaction with
Kirby, but I'm here to say that she reported details from my
past of which Shannon was still unaware. And why would
she wait seven years after we met. I am also not gullible,
perhaps the least likely person to believe blindly what I'm
told; life has proven that people are basically dishonest and
not to be believed. But I concede that my story sounds
highly improbable and even crazy, which creates my own
personal paradox.

My marriage to a psychic medium doesn't lead me to
automatically believe in all things paranormal. Over the
years I have seen Shannon deliver many accurate readings

for total strangers, situations in which gathering prior information would be impossible. In fact, Shannon's style of reading lends itself to total believability. She does not ask questions to pry information out of the subject, she simply begins talking and telling the person what the spirit is communicating to her, information that is very detailed and personal. Shannon is the real deal! Shannon stands to gain nothing making something like this up. She already has me and we are still both in love and if anything, Shannon and I will lose some of our privacy over this book which we both hold very dear, so why would Kirby's reading excel beyond the normal boundaries of a typical reading?

In the beginning, Kirby's desire to help me heal motivated him to contact me through Shannon. His appreciation to Shannon for allowing him to coexist with her on such a personal level proved the driving force behind Kirby sharing his knowledge of the afterlife with us. Kirby also apologized for it taking so long to deliver his message to me, but destiny controlled the timing of it. Destiny is the event that triggers the major events in our lives, while we maintain control over the minor ones. Kirby also told us we would wake up the day after the reading in disbelief, because the information we were given is so incredible. And he was right. The next day I was so wound up and bouncing off the walls with an energy that came from being the recipient of so much insight, but at the same time I felt conflicted. I realized then and now that many people will find it difficult to accept the truth behind Kirby's message. But at the end of the day, there is nothing I can do about what other people think or believe.

Kirby did tell us this book would not only change our lives, but many others as well. Most people are not atheist, believing at least in a higher power though discouraged with traditional religions because of money, power, corruption, scandals, wars, hypocritical behavior, numerous strict rules to live by and various other reasons. And this is not the only group Kirby said the book will connect with, a percentage of people who are already religious and or spiritual will connect with this book because *Living Beyond Existence* will help to tie all religions, spiritual beliefs, and science together into a more cohesive and understanding philosophy that will help unite and elevate more people to a higher spiritual level. Kirby claimed that a percentage of people will look at this book as an attack on religion, but many more will realize it is not against religion per say but against what people have done and continue to do with religion, including the very people who have written the worlds various religions. Originally, the message of religion was pure and accurate, but when written that message has been corrupted with extensive hierarchical, cultural, and gender points of view that distract from the true purpose of religion: a belief in a Supreme Being and in life after death, and not what is written from an earthbound point of view. Along this line, Kirby warned that the knowledge gained from his message must *not* be used to promote a personal agenda or to force those personal agendas onto other people. The point of his communication, as in life itself, centers on personal inner growth. Over time religions became a tool for dividing the world instead of unifying it. People who engage in this behavior are completely missing the point, or they see religion as a subject for manipulation to their personal advantage. My personal hope is that this book, and the message contained within it, be simply used as a self help guide for those people in need of it, and *not* as a new religion for manipulation by unscrupulous people.

∞

It's now 3:30 am on October 10th, and Kirby informs me his time here is running out. I have time for a last question, if I want to ask. I suppose I was numb from the overwhelming experience of the past five hours. My mind drew a literal blank. So how did this incredible reading with Kirby come to an end? As Shannon and I sat in shock and disbelief from the information made available to us; and with time running out I looked at Shannon and asked if Kirby wanted to ask me anything before he left us. All of a sudden, I see Kirby's smile manifested through Shannon's face, a painfully familiar and much-missed smile, and in a recognizable tone Kirby said, simply, "I love you, Bryon." I can't say that statement surprised me, but it was unexpectedly personal and touching in the context of the deep metaphysical topics covered throughout that night. Memories flooded over me, deeply-felt emotions surged, and all of the pain in my life including the day Kirby died welled up inside me. My eyes filled with tears, and for the first time since Kirby's death, the tears that I now cried were tears of happiness.

We are the beneficiaries of our yesterdays,

And the stewards of our tomorrows,

Let's do better to avoid being our own victims today.

Bryon Richard Smith

Chapter Nine

Shannon's Epiphany

As the psychic medium who channeled Kirby, I have a unique perspective to share with you regarding that night in October. That reading was very different from any other reading I had ever done before, because this time instead of just interpreting the information I was channeling Kirby, I was actually sharing my essence with him, and I could feel myself there but still separated for a portion of the reading. But during another part of the reading Kirby began to show me a series of images along with the knowledge on how the afterlife actually worked.

This is how *"The Souls of Existence"* was given to me. Personally I have always seen things psychically as if being shown through a thin veil, but not this time. What we have shared in this book is what came through to me that night. I would like to say I was as excited as my husband, Bryon, but later that day other messages were coming through warning me the knowledge we had learned should not have been shared with us.

These messages caused me both distress and confusion. I am one who believes in visions and the ones sent to me were pretty cut and dry. The first vision was of me standing on the banks of the river Styx, and before me was the cloaked ferryman Charon as he stood at the helm of his boat waiting to take my soul. Another vision was of a dark female in a warm glow pointing to a black light which represented my death. I took these images to be warnings not to follow through with this book, because what had been learned was not for us to know or to share. But logic told me we *have* been given a gift, a gift to be passed on to others. I have spent my entire life with a psychic gift that's been passed down from mother to daughter throughout generations, but I am the first one to carry the gift of a *medium*.

Over the years I have conducted many readings without anything like this happening, so why on that night did Kirby choose to show me so much more? In part, it was Kirby's appreciation to me for allowing him to channel through me in such a personal way, but also because he trusted Bryon to follow through with the writing of this book. And even though it is forbidden, maybe now is the time in our history that the information is needed. I just hope it provides for those who do need it the same healing Bryon received, a sense of healing from the loss of his cousin Kirby and an understanding to the long and painful emptiness he has felt most of his life. He has become a changed man. More complete, happier, less stressed, and most of all embracing a sense of purpose that has called out to him his whole life, once elusive, but is now finally found.

BEHIND THE MEDIUM

I am third generation Scots-Irish, my Grandmother Sheila Teal and Great Grandmother Janet Simpson always said there was something special about me. They were speaking psychically. I never knew what they meant until I was eleven. That is the year my Great Grandfather John Simpson, who was my best friend died. We would spend long hours fishing, watching Disney, and stealing snacks from my Great Grandmother's fridge when he was alive. He was the first spirit to ever come to me. Ironically enough this did not seem strange to me when it happened because his appearances seemed very clear and real to me, it would be many years later before I would realize what was psychically happening.

Throughout my teenage years and into my twenties I would see apparitions and hear voices but didn't quite know what to do about it. But then the true extent of my gift revealed itself in my thirties. The magic of my Great Grandfather being with me had long past and the logic of the real world had set in. Sometimes it was very frightening. Oddly enough, when my family would come across a haunted location, I was capable of communicating with the spirits so I could tell the story behind the haunting which would amaze them because the information I would relate to them were facts that could be later authenticated. Then in my early thirties spirits did not just show up at haunted locations anymore. They began to appear with people and were persistent about communicating with them through me. It was then I began to understand the depth of my gift, I was a medium, a *psychic medium*!

So I began to do readings for random strangers because the spirits who were with them were so persistent to be heard and I felt compelled to deliver those messages to help these people heal. And no, I did not charge for readings back then. Kirby was one such spirit who was very persistent and key in introducing me to my current husband Bryon, and that's when I began to truly blossom as a psychic medium.

Every moment leads us to where we're supposed to be.

Shannon Amy Smith

Author Biographies

Bryon (pronounced Brian) was born in Fremont, California and has lived throughout Northern California. He also lived in Albuquerque, New Mexico, for two years. He was born in Washington Hospital, graduated from Washington High, and is currently married to his second wife who is from Washington State ... how's that for karma? He is the author of the seven *Poems from Purgatory Series* of poetry books, a book of science fiction titled *The Destiny Trilogy*, another trilogy about teenage psychics titled *The Paranormals*, and also the *Trolley the Tarantula* series of children's books. Also two more stories are being written titled *The Ethereals* and *The Moaning Diaries*. All are planned to be published.

Shannon was born in Renton, Washington and raised throughout Washington State, living in Sunnyvale, California, for two years as a teenager before her family moved back to Washington. Shannon is a very gifted psychic medium as well as a very talented writer-poet in her own right. Her poetry is highlighted in the first two *Purgatory Series* of poetry books, which includes a poem entitled *How God Made Red* based on her oldest daughter Kali. She is also the author of two children's books titled

Timid Tina and Scaredy Cow, and *Cassie the Artist*, the latter being inspired by her youngest daughter of the same name. All are planned to be published.

Bryon and Shannon have been together since May of 2001, were hand fasted in August of 2002, and were married in August of 2003. They currently live in the Bay Area in Northern California. Shannon has been writing off and on throughout most of her life, while Bryon only started writing full time in September of 2008.

The End

Living Beyond Existence
Kirby's Gift from the Afterlife

And

The Purgatory Series:

Poems from Purgatory

Poems for Your Pleasure

Poems of Perception

Poems of Perfection

Poems of Persuasion

Poems that are Preferred

Poems in No Particular Order

********Are available at********

Amazon.com

In Print and Kindle Editions

Visit us on Facebook and YouTube

Kirby's Gift from the Afterlife

Living Beyond Existence

Kirby's Gift from the Afterlife

CPSIA information can be obtained at www.ICGtesting.com
Printed in the USA
LVOW120022180113

316161LV00024B/1306/P